TODAY'S U.S. NATIONAL GUARD

by KAREN LATCHANA KENNEY

Consultant:
Raymond L. Puffer, PhD
Historian, Retired
Edwards Air Force Base History Office

COMPASS POINT BOOKS
a capstone imprint

Compass Point Books are published by Capstone,
1710 Roe Crest Drive, North Mankato, Minnesota 56003
www.capstonepub.com

Editorial Credits
Managing Editor: Catherine Neitge
Designer: Alison Thiele
Production Specialist: Eric Manske
Library Consultant: Kathleen Baxter

Photo Credits
Air National Guard photo, 11; DoD photo by Matthew J. Wilson, U.S. Army, 21, Staff Sgt. Eric
Harris, USAF, 33, Staff Sgt. Stacy L. Pearsall, USAF, 26; Library of Congress, LC-DIG-pga-01949,
42; Louisiana Army and Air National Guard photo by Sgt 1st Class Paul Meeker, 7; New Jersey Air
National Guard photo by Tech Sgt. Matt Hecht, 13; North Dakota National Guard photo by Senior
Master Sgt. David Lipp, 9; Photo by Staff Sgt. Andrew H. Owen, Virginia Guard Public Affairs,
6; Photo by Staff Sgt. Tate Petersen, Company C, 2nd-135th General Support Aviation Support, 5;
Tennessee Army National Guard photo by Sgt. 1st Class Russell Klika, 39; U.S. Air Force photo by
Maj. Brandon Lingle, cover (top), Master Sgt. John Nimmo Sr., 18, Senior Master Sgt. Ray Lloyd,
30, Senior Master Sgt. Anthony L. Taylor, 22, Senior Master Sgt. David H. Lipp, 35, Staff Sgt. Dallas
Edwards, 41, Staff Sgt. Jeffrey T. Barone, cover (bottom), 1, 34, Staff Sgt. Michael B. Keller, 25, Tech
Sgt. Burke Baker, 27, Tech Sgt. Caycee Cook, 16, Tech Sgt. Sandra Niedzwiecki, 43, Tech Sgt. Steve
Faulisi, 29; U.S. Army photo by Frank Trevino, 31, Maj. Todd Harrell, 37, Sgt. Rebecca Linder, 15

Artistic Effects
Shutterstock: doodle, Ewa Walicka, Kilmukhametov Art, W.J.

Library of Congress Cataloging-in-Publication Data
Kenney, Karen Latchana.
  Today's U.S. National Guard / by Karen Latchana Kenney.
     p. cm—(The U.S. Armed Forces)
  Includes index.
  ISBN 978-0-7565-4619-9 (library binding)
  ISBN 978-0-7565-4639-7 (paperback)
  ISBN 978-0-7565-4675-5 (ebook PDF)
1. United States—National Guard. 2. United States—National Guard—Vocational guidance.
I. Title.
  UA42.K39 2013
  355.3'70973—dc23   2012031828

Printed in the United States of America in Brainerd, Minnesota.
092012   006938BANGS13

TABLE OF CONTENTS

CHAPTER ONE:
ALWAYS READY, ALWAYS THERE

It was extremely hot, dry, and windy—a menacing combination—in Colorado Springs, Colorado. The weather provided perfect conditions for the devastating wildfires that were quickly spreading through the area in June 2012. As the fires raged, National Guard members rushed by land and air to help. Some were Coloradans. Others came from Nebraska, Kansas, and Wyoming. Guard members flew UH-60 Black Hawk helicopters over the fires, dropping 500 gallons (1,893 liters) of water at a time from each aircraft. On the ground, Guard members used special firefighting trucks they call "beasts" to fight the blaze.

The Waldo Canyon fire entered Colorado Springs on June 26. By the next day, more than 32,000 people had been evacuated from the area. "The fire conditions could not be worse," said Anne Rys-Sikora, spokeswoman for a fire-response team. "It is like a convection oven out there." More National Guard members arrived to help contain the fire, assist with police-run roadblocks, and patrol the streets.

The wildfire was the most destructive in Colorado history. By the time it was contained July 10, two people had died, close to 350 homes were destroyed, and more than 18,000 acres (7,284 hectares)

of land were scorched.

Being prepared to respond quickly is what the National Guard is about. Its motto, "Always Ready, Always There," explains it all. The National Guard is a branch of the U.S. armed forces that trains regularly but is only called to active duty when needed. Sergeant 1st Class John Schreiber, a fire chief and first sergeant

Nebraska National Guardsmen dropped water from a helicopter's bucket onto a Colorado wildfire.

with the Colorado Army National Guard's 1157th Engineer Firefighter Company, said Guardsmen interrupt their lives in emergencies to help others.

"I have a soldier who is missing a wedding," he said. "Another soldier has a landscaping business that's on hold, and one is missing a job interview, and not one of them has complained. They're 100 percent volunteers. These are the kinds of personalities we draw. Every time you see them, they're just happy to do their job. It's a passion."

Guard members were also ready and willing to serve when hurricanes hit the U.S. East Coast. Hurricane Irene in 2011 and Hurricane Sandy in 2012 brought high winds, torrential rain, and storm surges. They caused power outages, demolished homes, and flooded streets and highways. They affected millions of people. Many were stranded without food, fresh water, or medical care. They needed help quickly.

Thousands of Guard members immediately responded to the disasters.

Virginia Guardsmen were at the ready when Hurricane Irene hit.

Louisiana Guardsmen attached sandbags to a helicopter.

They helped people in East Coast states, from North Carolina to Maine. They cleared debris, filled sandbags, and assessed damage. They performed search-and-rescue missions. They helped control traffic and handed out cots, food, and supplies. The National Guard brought not only help but also hope that things would soon return to normal.

7

CITIZEN SOLDIERS

The volunteers who are always ready and able to help during national emergencies are part of a unique branch of the military. The U.S. National Guard is made of two main forces—the Air National Guard and the Army National Guard.

In both, members split their time between civilian and military lives. Unlike members of other military branches, National Guard members work part time for the military. That is why they are sometimes called citizen soldiers.

BY THE NUMBERS

In 2012 there were 358,200 members of the Army National Guard and 106,700 members of the Air National Guard, according to the National Guard Bureau.

The Air National Guard provides air support for state and national missions. It provides air defense of the United States and national disaster relief, and it supports the Air Force in many ways. The support includes aerial refueling, medical evacuations, and emergency relief during floods, forest fires, and earthquakes. The Air National Guard has 89 flying units and 579 mission-support units.

The Army National Guard also supports state and national missions. When called upon for national missions, the Army Guard may be sent to various parts of the world to support military operations. State missions include support during or after storms, floods, or civil disturbances, such as riots.

Each state, the Commonwealth of Puerto Rico, the territories of Guam and the Virgin Islands, and the District of Columbia has a National Guard. Governors command each state's or territory's National Guard, and a general runs the National Guard in Washington, D.C. A governor or the general can order troops into action for support in an emergency. During national emergencies, the U.S. president can order Guard troops into action.

National Guard members are not always taking part in military action. They have civilian jobs and live at home. But they also train regularly for military action. They are ready when called upon to support their states and nation. They are always there when needed and are an important branch of the U.S. armed forces.

Members of the North Dakota Guard boarded a flight that would take them to service in Southwest Asia.

THE OLDEST BRANCH

● ● ● ● ● ● ● ● ● ● ● ● ●

The National Guard is the oldest branch of the U.S. armed forces. It traces its beginnings to the English colonies of North America. The colonists brought the English system of local militias with them. This system required all males ages 16 to 60 to carry arms and defend their communities if necessary. In December 1636 the first organized militia was created, in Massachusetts Bay Colony. The early militias trained once a week. They also guarded their communities each night, watching for danger.

Militias protected the colonies from local attacks. They also helped the United States win the Revolutionary War (1775–1783) against Great Britain. After the war the U.S. Constitution gave Congress the ability to provide supplies and weapons to state militias. It also gave the states power to appoint officers to the militias and train their members. This was the beginning of the Guard's dual state and national roles.

Militias became known as the National Guard in 1903. Legislation increased the Guard's role in support of the U.S. Army. Some Guard aviation units were used during World War I (1914–1918). After

World War II (1939–1945), some of those units were formed into the Air National Guard. Through the years both the Army and Air National Guard have helped the United States achieve victory in battle.

Private Beckwith Havens flew the first National Guard aerial mission in 1912.

CHAPTER TWO:
NATIONAL GUARD CAREERS

The thousands of men and women who make up the National Guard have many career paths to follow—from being dental specialists to being cannon operators. There are more than 150 jobs to choose from in the Army National Guard and more than 200 in the Air National Guard. Certain jobs are only for men, and other jobs are for both men and women. Many Guard jobs provide experience that not only is valuable to the military but also can transfer to civilian careers.

The infantry is the main ground force of the Army National Guard. These jobs are only available to men.

Infantrymen are trained to use weapons and in hand-to-hand combat. They also learn other combat and observational skills, and how to serve in peacekeeping forces. Some infantrymen learn how to use mines, scout enemy locations, and make firing positions. Infantrymen gain skills in leadership, teamwork, and discipline.

There are various specialties in armor and field artillery careers. These soldiers operate tanks, cannons, and missile launchers. These large weapons support infantry and tank units in combat. Some jobs in this part of the Guard focus on gathering and reporting information about

the enemy and monitoring weather
conditions to aid the missile launchers.
Of the 13 armor and field artillery jobs,
three are open to women. Some skills
that can transfer to civilian jobs include
technology support and mechanics.

A member of the New Jersey
Air National Guard
maintenance squadron
straps down munitions at an
airfield in Afghanistan.

There are many aviation jobs in both the Army and Air National Guard. In the Air National Guard, members can fly aircraft, be flight attendants, or do in-flight refueling with other aircraft. Maintaining helicopters, operating aerial weapons, and engineering are other jobs. Many of the 16 career categories in the Air National Guard are not directly related to aircraft. These careers teach a wide variety of skills that can be applied to civilian jobs. All jobs in the Air National Guard are open to men and women. Aviation jobs in the Army National Guard include 21 specialties. Among them are working as an aircraft electrician or an air traffic control operator.

There are many medical career options in both the Air and Army National Guard. Health care specialists provide emergency and basic medical care. Mental health workers treat patients with substance abuse or psychological problems. Some medical specialists inspect food before it is cooked and served to soldiers. Medical jobs are open to men and women and provide many skills that easily transfer to civilian jobs in the health care industry.

Military police are the police force on Army or Guard property. They investigate crimes and accidents, control traffic, and help with emergencies. They also protect senior officers and deal with prisoners of war on the battlefield. The jobs are open to men and women, and skills learned can transfer to careers in law enforcement and security.

A nurse (left) and physician's assistant treat a simulated casualty during a National Guard exercise in Afghanistan.

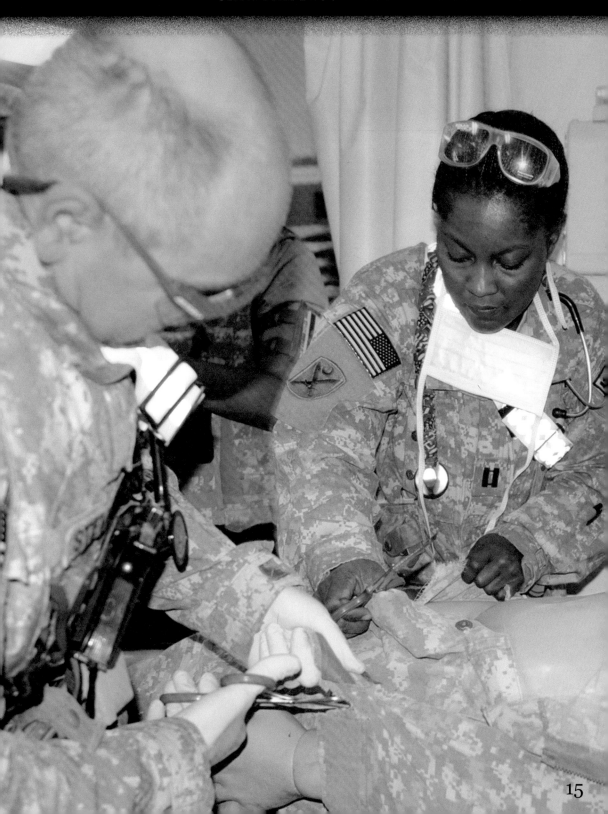

Intelligence specialists help the Army and Air National Guard gather and use important information. They use high-tech equipment, such as satellites, computers, and radios, to collect and analyze information. Some specialists interpret messages, and others maintain and set up the equipment. In the Air Guard, highly trained specialists operate remotely piloted aircraft.

Interpreters and translators are also valued workers in the Guard. They speak foreign languages and help officers communicate with people in other countries. Their skills can transfer to civilian jobs in research, interpretation, and communication companies.

Transportation, logistics, and mechanic and maintenance jobs are found in both the Army and Air National Guard. These workers help transfer soldiers and airmen and their equipment where they are needed. They make sure that Guard units have the supplies they need to complete their jobs. And they make sure the tools Guard members use work well. Some of these jobs are working in kitchens, driving trucks and buses, and fixing power generators. The jobs are open to men and women and provide skills needed for many civilian jobs.

MOVING UP THE RANKS

As a soldier or airman gains more National Guard experience and education and performs well on duty, he or she can be awarded a higher rank. In the Army Guard, the lowest rank is private and the highest rank is general. In the Air Guard, the lowest rank is airman basic and the highest rank is general.

A South Carolina Guardsman in a maintenance squadron unloads ammunition while on duty in Iraq.

The Special Forces are for elite soldiers in the Army and Army National Guard. Open only to men, these jobs are for high achieving soldiers who perform challenging and often dangerous missions. They may jump from planes at 30,000 feet (9,144 meters) or enter hostile waters without being seen or heard. The

Colorado Army National Guard Special Forces soldiers fired their M-4 carbines at a target during an excercise.

requirements for these jobs are tougher than for other jobs in the Guard. But once in, these elite Guardsmen can be involved in important missions.

Both the Air and Army National Guard need engineers. These specialists construct buildings and other structures needed by Guard units. They may work on basic construction and electrical and plumbing jobs. Or they may survey land or draft maps or plans for buildings. Some work on bridges, dams, or airfields. Most jobs are open to men and women, and their skills can lead to civilian jobs in architecture, construction, and electrical engineering.

Those working in the administrative field do the behind-the-scenes work in the Army and Air National Guard. These specialists work in offices maintaining records, writing letters, handling the payrolls, and doing other office duties. Public affairs Guard members write and edit news stories, take photos, and distribute radio and TV programming. A paralegal assistant works with judges, lawyers, and commanders

on legal work. Men and women in these jobs gain a wide variety of skills that apply to many civilian jobs, including news broadcaster, accountant, and human resources worker.

Besides the many skills learned on the job and the salaries earned in the Guard, there are added benefits. Guard members receive money for college. They can receive tuition money, a monthly college allowance, and money for books and supplies and payment of student loans. Certain high-demand jobs offer cash bonuses. Other benefits include free flights on military aircraft within the United States, help in qualifying for home loans, and low-cost health insurance.

MONEY FOR SCHOOL

The National Guard provides up to $18,000 of tuition money, split over four years, to Guard members. State contributions can bring the total to $40,000.

19

CHAPTER THREE:
JOINING THE GUARD

Not everyone can join the National Guard. Physical strength is important, but it is not everything. Applicants must meet strict requirements to join the Guard. They must pass a series of tests as well. Only then can they be considered for enlistment.

Applicants usually must be U.S. citizens, but some citizens of other countries who are legal residents of the U.S. can also apply. They also must be the right age—from 17 to 40 to join the Air National Guard and from 17 to 35 to join the Army National Guard. Most states and territories require that applicants have high school diplomas or are working toward GED (general educational development) certificates.

There are also moral requirements. A person who has been convicted of a serious crime will not be accepted into the Guard. If the applicant has a history of trouble with the law, that person may not qualify. A person also may not qualify for medical reasons, such as blood diseases, problems moving limbs and hands, or heart disease. Addiction to drugs or alcohol may disqualify a person from enlisting.

Potential Guard members who meet the basic requirements can visit a Guard representative called a recruiter. A recruiter answers the person's questions, and they discuss whether the Guard is the right fit for the person. If both agree that the Guard is a good fit, the person moves along in the enlistment process.

The next step is to take the Armed Services Vocational Aptitude Battery (ASVAB). This test measures applicants'

A Missouri National Guard soldier leaps from a rappel tower during training.

knowledge in eight areas. They include math, science, word knowledge, electronics, mechanics, and automotive and wood shop skills. The ASVAB determines an applicant's strengths. This helps the Guard direct him or her on the best career path. The test can be taken at schools or military testing or processing stations. It takes about three and a half hours to complete.

Recruits were inducted into the Army National Guard during halftime of a University of Tennessee-Vanderbilt football game.

After receiving passing ASVAB results, applicants pick the jobs they would like to have. They can meet with a recruiter and discuss their options.

Applicants must also pass a version of the Army physical fitness test. It measures the number of sit-ups and push-ups applicants can do in a set time. They must also run up to 2 miles (3.2 kilometers) within a certain time to pass. There are height and weight requirements. These physical tests and requirements make sure the person is ready for the physical demands of military service.

Applicants then go to a Military Entrance Processing Station (MEPS) for physical exams by military doctors. They also speak with jobs counselors and make final job selections. They lock in a date to leave for basic training. And they take their oath of enlistment, making them official members of the National Guard. Enlistees agree to serve in the Army National Guard for eight

years or the Air National Guard for six years. The enlistment period can be split between active duty and reserve status.

The next stop for the new members of the National Guard is basic training. But it may be a while before they leave. New Army Guardsmen enter a recruit sustainment program while they wait. Air Guardsmen enter a delayed entry program. During the waiting period, the new recruits meet regularly to learn Guard rules and organization. They also start fitness and classroom training. Recruits prepare for the challenges of basic training ahead.

TAKING THE OATH

Every member of the National Guard swears an oath to uphold two constitutions, the U.S. Constitution and the state or territory constitution.

CHAPTER FOUR:
BASIC TRAINING

The rigors of basic training transform new recruits into soldiers and airmen. In those weeks of training, they will become mentally and physically stronger. They will become prepared to serve in the military.

For the Army National Guard, Basic Combat Training lasts 10 weeks. Training centers are in five places: Fort Benning in Georgia; Fort Jackson in South Carolina; Fort Knox in Kentucky; Fort Leonard Wood in Missouri; and Fort Sill in Oklahoma. In the Air Guard, Basic Military Training lasts eight weeks at Lackland Air Force Base in Texas.

In the weeks of training, recruits are tested both physically and mentally. They become stronger and tougher, learn to follow commands and use weapons, and learn about the military way of life.

Training starts with orientation, called Zero Week. Male recruits are given short haircuts. Women are told how to wear their hair—above their collars or high and tight in buns. Recruits receive physical exams and shots. They also receive their uniforms. Zero Week becomes a new starting point for recruits. During this week they get an introduction to their training. They start practicing teamwork and learn dorm and drill basics. They get ready for the real training to begin in Week One.

For the Army Guard, training has three phases. The red phase lasts three weeks. First comes the shakedown—recruits meet their drill sergeant, who teaches them many of the skills needed to become soldiers. The drill sergeant tests

Recruits take part in combat training at Fort Jackson.

the recruits' abilities to follow orders. Recruits are ordered to line up their bags in a certain way and then empty them. If they do this incorrectly, they quickly learn the punishment for not following orders. Drill sergeants are not only teachers but also strict disciplinarians.

During the red phase, Guard members learn about the Army's core values, how to assemble and care for their rifles, first aid, and basic combat techniques. They have fitness training, and they learn about discipline and teamwork. Air Guard recruits learn similar skills.

Then comes the white phase, which lasts two weeks and is known as the gunfighter phase. Combat skills are taught, including using weapons, and there is more physical training. Soldiers learn how to use their rifles and participate in night training. They learn how to read compasses and maps. Air Guard members receive antiterrorism training and learn how to mentally prepare for combat, among other skills.

The final phase, which lasts four weeks, is called the warrior phase. Army Guard training continues with weapon use and various kinds of military operations. This phase includes tests that recruits must pass in order to graduate. The End of Cycle Test includes 212 tasks that recruits must

Shuffling down a rope obstacle course is part of combat training.

successfully perform. Recruits must pass the Army physical fitness test. Air Guard recruits also continue their training and take written and physical tests.

Graduation week ends basic training for all recruits. They finish their final training, spend time with their families, and attend their graduation ceremonies. But their rest is brief. Soon the new soldiers and airmen will move on to their individualized training. There they will learn the specific skills needed for the careers they have been assigned. After basic training, National Guard members have shared an experience and have prepared physically and mentally for combat. They feel like true members of the military.

CHAPTER FIVE:
GEAR AND EQUIPMENT

The weapons, vehicles, and gear recruits learn about in basic training are the important tools Guard members use in battle and disaster relief. It is the same gear and equipment used in the U.S. Army and Air Force. It keeps Guard members safe and helps them accomplish their important missions.

The Guard uses a number of ground vehicles. Some are wheeled, such as trucks, and some are tracked, such as tanks. Many types of trucks are used to move cargo, heavy equipment, and Guard members. Some of the larger trucks can hold up to 5 tons (4.5 metric tons) of cargo. Some trucks are designed to travel over minefields. Mine Resistant Ambush Protected vehicles have V-shaped hulls and armor plating to keep troops inside safe from bullets, exploding bombs, and mines. Tracked vehicles, such as M113 armored vehicles, are made to travel over battlefields. They are protected with walls of armor.

STRONG BUT SLOW

The M88A2 Hercules aids in battlefield recovery missions. The powerful vehicle has a draw bar, winch, and boom that can lift and tow other tanks and combat vehicles. The Hercules weighs 70 tons (64 metric tons) and can lift or pull its own weight. But all that weight makes it a slow vehicle. Its top speed with a load is 17 miles (27 km) per hour.

Armed soldiers leave the back of an M113 armored personnel carrier while on duty in northern Iraq.

WIDE RANGE OF AIRCRAFT • • • • • • • • • • • • •

The C-130 Hercules (above) is a commonly used cargo plane. It has four engines and can carry up to 44,000 pounds (20,000 kilograms). It has a crew of three to five and can hold up to 128 fully armed troops.

The F-16 Fighting Falcon is a fighter airplane. It is used in air-to-air combat and air-to-ground attacks. A bubble canopy over the cockpit gives the pilot clear views all around the plane.

The CH-47 Chinook helicopter is another key aircraft. It can transport ground forces, supplies, ammunition, and other cargo. It has a maximum speed of 184 mph (296 kph).

Aircraft are used for a variety of reasons in the Guard. They engage in combat, transport cargo, refuel other aircraft in flight, deliver weapons, and support firefighting and natural disaster missions. National Guard aircraft include airplanes and helicopters.

Weapons used by the Guard range from rifles, pistols, knives, and machine guns to missile systems. The M-16 rifle is a magazine-fed rifle that is made for accurate direct fire. The M-240B machine gun is mounted on the ground. It can shoot from 200 to 600 rounds per minute. The Patriot missile can intercept attacking aircraft and missiles as far as 50 miles (80 km) away. The TOW (Tube-launched, Optically-tracked, Wire command-link) anti-armor missile system was introduced in 1970. It can be mounted on various types of vehicles, including helicopters and Humvees. It can fire at a range of 12,300 feet (3,750 m).

The MIM-104 Patriot is a surface-to-air missile system.

Guard members wear special gear in battle. When needed, a field mask protects a Guard member's face and eyes from chemical and biological agents, radioactive particles, and other contaminants. It has many features that allow it to be worn for eight to 12 hours straight. A special suit can be worn with the mask to protect the entire body from the same contaminants. It is light, comes in two pieces, and is made from state-of-the-art materials. Carbon in the suit's liner can absorb chemical agents. Guard members use a special kit that can detect chemical agents. The kit helps them find chemical agents and to know when they can remove their masks and suits.

The many tools provided to Guard members help them stay safe and accomplish what is asked of them. Such a wide variety of tools is needed because missions take them to many places. The Guard also provides widely varying services on their missions—from fighting forest fires to assisting troops in battle.

South Carolina Guardsmen wear protective suits during a training exercise.

CHAPTER SIX:
ASSIGNMENTS AND MISSIONS

When the National Guard is called into action, it is for one of four reasons—disaster relief, homeland defense, combat action, or a national emergency. The governor of a state or territory can order the state or territory's Guard troops into action, which is often for disaster relief. But if there is a national need, such as a war or national emergency, the president can call the Guard into service.

Once the president activates the National Guard, it comes under the command of the Department of Defense. Each state or territory's Joint Force Headquarters coordinates the response of

Louisiana National Guardsmen worked through the night after an oil spill.

A National Guard helicopter dropped 1-ton sandbags during flood relief efforts in North Dakota.

the state's Air and Army National Guard. These headquarters are open 24 hours a day, seven days a week. They help states communicate with one another and the federal government and coordinate the deployment of the National Guard. They also work with the Department of Defense's U.S. Northern Command, which is in charge of homeland defense operations.

When the mission is disaster relief, the National Guard helps in many ways. The Guard has been called to action to deal with earthquakes, floods, tornadoes, and forest fires. When New Orleans was flooded after Hurricane Katrina in 2005, the Guard brought in food and vital supplies to people stranded in the city. And years later, when Hurricane Isaac hit the South and Hurricane Sandy hit the East Coast, the Guard was ready. After tornadoes ravaged 11 states in 2011, the Guard responded. Guard units helped people evacuate, searched for survivors, and delivered supplies. To fight the Colorado wildfires, the Guard used special fire trucks to reach remote areas. They also used remote-controlled water cannons to fight the huge fires. Guard medical support teams can erect temporary hospitals that can care for thousands of people. Whatever way they help, the overall goal is to restore peace, order, and normal functioning to devastated areas.

PROTECTION AT HOME

After the terrorist attacks on September 11, 2001, the National Guard started playing a larger role in homeland defense. Guard Reaction Forces can respond to threats within eight hours.

The Guard Reaction Forces can create roadblocks and checkpoints, assist with civil disturbances, and protect roads, bridges, and other structures. Civil Support Teams can determine whether there are weapons of mass destruction at a site. Other teams are ready to provide emergency assistance if weapons destroy buildings, roads, or bridges or cause other large-scale disasters. The teams offer medical, search-and-rescue, and decontamination support.

The Guard also participates in efforts against illegal drugs. About 2,500 soldiers and airmen work with state and federal governments to detect and stop the movement of drugs.

Guard members participating in the Southwest Border Mission have helped law enforcement agencies secure the border with Mexico to prevent illegal drugs from being smuggled into the United States. In November 2010 the Guard helped seize 50 tons (45 metric tons) of marijuana from tunnels under the Mexico-California border.

BOOTS ON THE GROUND

Just two weeks after Hurricane Katrina devastated New Orleans, more than 42,000 Army National Guard troops were in the area for disaster relief.

West Virginia Guard Reaction Forces trained in Washington, D.C.

The National Guard plays a role in national defense missions supporting U.S. troops in other countries. They are involved in peacekeeping or humanitarian missions in Kosovo, the Horn of Africa, and the Sinai Peninsula, and at the U.S. military detention facility in Guantanamo Bay, Cuba. State National Guard units are deployed in Afghanistan, Iraq, and Kuwait.

The National Guard is involved in a wide variety of missions and assignments. Its help during natural disasters restores normality to people's lives. Its ability to quickly respond to national emergencies saves lives. This kind of flexibility makes the Guard a valuable part of the military.

Guardsmen trained in Mississippi before their deployment to Iraq.

FINDING A HOME IN THE GUARD

Sergeant Alyssa Vasquez joined the Army National Guard of Tennessee when she was 17 years old. She was attracted by the benefits she saw in Guard service: tuition assistance, work experience, and more. When Vasquez had the opportunity to leave the Guard, she decided to stay for one more year. That year she voluntarily went to Iraq as part of a national defense mission. Vasquez said:

"It was not until I found myself in another country, with thousands of people who all believed in one common cause, that I realized why I belonged in the National Guard. I joined the Guard because of what I wanted from it, but I stayed in the National Guard because I found a home in my fellow soldiers. Finding that home gave me the strength to want to give back to my community, country, and comrades."

CHAPTER SEVEN:
LEADERS IN THE GUARD

To accomplish the National Guard's many important missions throughout the centuries, great leaders have played key roles. They have led troops through tough assignments on U.S. and foreign soil. These leaders, along with the courageous service of their troops, have contributed to the Guard's outstanding reputation.

An early leader was George Washington, who was an officer in the Virginia militia when he was only 20 years old. Washington went on to have a celebrated military career and to become the first U.S. president.

Washington was the first of 20 U.S. presidents to serve in the National Guard. They include Thomas Jefferson, Abraham Lincoln, Ulysses S. Grant, Theodore Roosevelt, and Harry S. Truman. The most recent president who served in the Guard was George W. Bush. He was also the only president to have served in the Air National Guard.

An Arizona soldier patrols in Afghanistan, one of many countries served by the National Guard.

Militiamen stormed Fort Wagner during the Civil War (1861–1865).

A famous militia unit was the 54th Massachusetts Volunteer Infantry Regiment. It was the first northern regiment made up of African-American soldiers to fight in the Civil War. Many whites at the time did not believe African-Americans could be good soldiers. But the 54th regiment proved them wrong. They fought bravely and suffered many casualties in their attack on Fort Wagner, South Carolina, in 1863. Their story was told in the Academy Award-winning movie *Glory.*

Another celebrated Guardsman was Hank Gowdy. He was the only active Major League Baseball player/coach to serve in two world wars. A hero of the 1914 World Series, when he helped the Boston Braves to a four-game sweep of the Philadelphia Athletics, Gowdy proved

U.S. GRANT

Ulysses S. Grant became one of the most famous military leaders in American history. As colonel of an Illinois militia unit during the Civil War, Grant was given the nickname "Unconditional Surrender Grant" after he refused to negotiate with a southern general in 1862. Under his leadership, the Union Army defeated Confederate forces to win the Civil War. Grant later served as U.S. president.

to be a real hero during World War I. In 1917 he joined the Ohio National Guard and was sent to the front lines in France. His infantry commander called him one of his top men. During World War II, while working as a coach with the Cincinnati Reds, Gowdy volunteered for Army service but was rejected. Then the following year, 1943, he received a commission as an Army captain and served stateside. He resumed his coaching career in 1945.

With its great leaders and dedicated soldiers and airmen, the National Guard is an invaluable part of the U.S. armed forces. Whether it is needed within hours after a natural disaster or to support troops on longer missions abroad, the National Guard is always ready to be called into action. It is there when Americans need it the most.

An F-15 Eagle under the watchful eye of an Air National Guardsman

GLOSSARY

ammunition: bullets and other objects that can be fired from weapons

civilian: person who is not in the military

contaminant: substance that is poisonous or harmful to the human body

decontamination: removal of harmful substances from some thing or place

deploy: to move troops into position for military action

enlist: to voluntarily join a branch of the military

evacuate: to move people away from a threatened or dangerous place to somewhere safer

humanitarian: concerned with ending the suffering of others

militia: group of citizens who are trained to fight, but who only serve in an emergency; the National Guard serves as the militia for the United States

morals: beliefs about what is right and wrong

orientation: program of introduction to a school or job

peacekeeping: active maintenance of a truce between nations or communities, especially by an international military force

recruiter: military member who provides guidance to people interested in joining the armed forces

weapons of mass destruction: chemical, biological, or radioactive weapons capable of causing widespread death and destruction

SOURCE NOTES

Chapter 1: Always Ready, Always There
Page 4, col. 2, line 4: Gast, Phil. "32,000 evacuated in fast-moving Colorado Springs wildfire." CNN. 26 June 2012. 30 Oct. 2012. www.cnn.com/2012/06/26/us/western-wildfires/index.html

Page 6, line 1: Theiral, Master Sgt. Cheresa D. "Outflanking the flames: Guardsmen, first responders continue integrated war against High Park fire." Colorado National Guard Public Affairs Office. 25 June 2012. 30 Oct. 2012. http://co.ng.mil/News/Pages/120625-02hpfirefirefighters.aspx

Chapter 6: Assignments and Missions
Page 39, line 1: Sgt. Alyssa Vasquez. Soldier Stories. National Guard. 30 Oct. 2012. www.nationalguard.com/guard-basics/soldier-stories/sgt-alyssa-vasquez

READ MORE

Palser, Barb. *Hurricane Katrina: Aftermath of Disaster.*
Minneapolis.: Compass Point Books, 2007.

Raatma, Lucia. *The Science of Soldiers.*
Mankato, Minn.: Compass Point Books, 2012.

Somervill, Barbara A. *First Response: By Air.*
New York: Children's Press, 2007.

INTERNET SITES

Use FactHound to find Internet sites related to this book. All of the sites on FactHound have been researched by our staff.

Here's all you do:

Visit *www.facthound.com*

Type in this code: 9780756546199

RESOURCES

The National Guard
www.nationalguard.mil
Official website of the National Guard offers information and links

Air National Guard
www.ang.af.mil/index.asp
Provides information about joining the Air National Guard

Army National Guard
www.arng.army.mil/Pages/Default.aspx
Provides information about joining the Army National Guard

TITLES IN THIS SERIES:

TODAY'S U.S. **AIR FORCE**

TODAY'S U.S. **ARMY**

TODAY'S U.S. **MARINES**

TODAY'S U.S. **NATIONAL GUARD**

TODAY'S U.S. **NAVY**

INDEX

ABOUT THE AUTHOR

Author and editor Karen Latchana Kenney has written many books for children and young adults. From the science of cars to the history of the Japanese-American internment during World War II, she has explored numerous topics in the writing and researching of her books. Kenney lives in Minneapolis, Minnesota, with her husband and young son.